Giuseppe Verdi

Pater noster

for unaccompanied SSATB choir

VOCAL SCORE

Edited by

JUDITH BLEZZARD
with an English translation by
Brian Trowell

Music Department
OXFORD UNIVERSITY PRESS
Oxford and New York

Oxford University Press, Walton Street, Oxford OX2 6DP
Oxford University Press, 198 Madison Avenue, New York, NY 10016, USA
Oxford New York
Athens Auckland Bangkok Bombay
Calcutta Cape Town Dar es Salaam Delhi
Florence Hong Kong Istanbul Karachi
Kuala Lumpur Madras Madrid Melbourne
Mexico City Nairobi Paris Singapore
Taipei Tokyo Toronto

and associated companies in
Berlin Ibadan

Oxford is a trade mark of Oxford University Press

9 10 8

ISBN 0 19 338432 9

Printed in Great Britain on acid-free paper by Halstan & Co. Ltd., Amersham, Bucks.

PREFACE

This Italian elaboration of the Lord's Prayer is attributed to Dante. It is similar in style and layout to a version of the Lord's Prayer in Canto XI, lines 1–24, of *Purgatorio* (the second of the three sections in Dante's *La Divina Commedia)*, where souls in the first of the seven circles of purgatory are making amends for the sin of pride. In both versions the prayer provides the framework for picturesque digressions of a devotional nature: elaborated paraphrases like these were a frequent literary product of medieval times. The resulting vivid and dramatic text is ideally matched by Verdi's colourful and emotive setting, composed in 1880 for unaccompanied five-part choir.

Apart from the well-known *Requiem* of 1874, very little of Verdi's choral music is performed in English-speaking countries. Though his choral output was small, it reflects much of the boldness and finesse of his finest opera choruses. There are only two pieces for unaccompanied choir apart from *Pater noster*: *Ave Maria* (1889, with subsequent revisions) for unaccompanied mixed choir—an ingenious exercise exploring the possibilities of an enigmatic chromatic scale; and *Laudi alla Vergine Maria (1890)* for two sopranos and two altos, on a text by Dante.

Text authorship is not the only common feature linking the *Laudi* with *Pater noster*. The colourful use of harmonic progressions (both expected and unexpected), the contrasts of dynamics and textures, and the moments of silence to heighten perception of the text are other shared characteristics. The superbly wrought digressions into remote keys as both pieces draw to a close are very much part of Verdi's meditative yet dramatic style. *Pater noster* can appropriately be used as part of a church service (in writing it Verdi was paying homage to the style of Palestrina's church music), but it is perhaps most effective as a concert piece: this was the composer's original intention.

Brief commentaries on the piece may be found in Julian Budden: *Verdi* (London, Dent, 1985) and Francis Toye: *Giuseppe Verdi: his life and works* (London, Heinemann, 1931). It was composed in 1880 and given its première at a benefit concert at La Scala. The present edition was made from the score and separate vocal parts published in the same year by G. Ricordi and Co., Milan. A few very minor inconsistencies, mostly concerned with accentuation in the music, have been rectified. Slight adjustments have been made to some of the dynamic markings: a small number that were superfluous have been omitted, and those that have been added editorially appear in square brackets. Clefs have been modernized, and a keyboard reduction (for rehearsal only) has been added. Of the voice-ranges supplied editorially at the opening, the lowest extreme of the bass applies only to bars 164–5, where the basses divide: use of the upper bass note only at this point does not damage the harmony, although the *divisi* is preferable if possible. The metronome mark is from the first edition.

Two performance indications may require comment. Verdi's ^ accents do not indicate the strong degree of attack that the symbol may imply to the modern eye, but merely a slightly percussive accentuation within the context of the prevailing dynamic. The direction *Portando la voce* at bar 130 (all voices except bass) means, literally, 'carrying the voice', synonymous with *portamento*, the expressive device of gliding lightly between one note and the next. For choral performance, the effect may need some rehearsal.

Two English translations are provided. Professor Brian Trowell's is intended for singing, and is interlined in the score. He comments that 'the original is written in *terza rima* (aba bcb cdc, etc.), and Verdi does observe the structure of the tercets (though Dante would have used a lyric form, not *terza rima*, if he had meant these verses to be sung). The text is partly a trope on the Lord's Prayer, but some of the additional words are inserted simply to produce a rhymed and metrical text. The translation can only rarely employ the traditional English Lord's Prayer, and is not too tightly bound to the precise meaning of Dante's insertions except where they are inescapably underlined by Verdi's music. It helps to keep some rhyme (the outer lines of each tercet), since the diction that results allows one to use older forms of diction familiar from the liturgy and to depart from everyday speech and word order, as in a hymn.'

The second translation is given below, with the Italian in its original form. This literal version, unconstrained by the needs of musical performance, is a closer reflection of the meaning of the text, and provides programme material for English-speaking audiences of choirs who prefer to sing the piece in Italian. I should like to acknowledge the help of Dr Graham Dixon with the draft translation, and also the invaluable expertise of Professor Michael Talbot in producing the final version of the literal translation and in helping me gain access to some of the necessary material.

JUDITH BLEZZARD
May 1995

TEXT AND TRANSLATION

O Padre nostro, che ne' cieli stai,
Santificato sia sempre il tuo nome,
E laude e grazia di ciò che ci fai.

Avvenga il regno tuo, siccome pone
Questa orazion: tua volontà si faccia,
Siccome in cielo, in terra in unione.

Padre, dà oggi a noi pane, e ti piaccia
Che ne perdoni li peccati nostri;
Nè cosa noi facciam che ti dispiaccia.

E che noi perdoniam, tu ti dimostri
Esempio a noi per la tua gran virtute;
Acciò dal rio nemico ognun si schiostri.

Divino Padre, pien d'ogni salute,
Ancor ci guarda dalla tentazione
Dell' infernal nemico e sue ferute.

Sì che a te facciamo orazione,
Che meritiam tua grazia, e il regno vostro
A posseder vegniam con divozione.

Preghiamti, re di gloria e signor nostro,
Che tu ci guardi da dolore: e fitto
La mente abbiamo in te, col volto prostro.

Amen.

Based on DANTE, *Purgatorio*, XI. 1–24

O our Father, who art in heaven,
hallowed be thy name always,
and praise and thanks be for everything that thou doest.

Thy kingdom come, as this prayer entreats:
Thy will be done,
On earth, as it is in heaven.

Father, give us this day our daily bread,
and may it please thee to forgive us our sins:
and let us not do anything that displeases thee.

And in order that we may forgive, thou makest thyself
an example to us through thy great goodness;
so that we can all escape from the cruel enemy.

Heavenly Father, fount of all salvation,
keep us always from temptation,
from the satanic enemy and his onslaughts.

As we pray to thee
that we may deserve thy grace
and that we may devoutly enter into thy kingdom,

we beg thee, King of Glory and our Lord,
to preserve us from sorrow: and we have
our minds fixed on thee, with head lowered.

Amen.

(Literal translation)

Pater Noster

The Lord's Prayer
Elaborated by Dante (1265–1321)
English translation by Brian Trowell

GIUSEPPE VERDI
(1813–1901)
Edited by Judith Blezzard

Printed in Great Britain

OXFORD UNIVERSITY PRESS, MUSIC DEPARTMENT, WALTON STREET, OXFORD OX2 6DP

15
mf
-to sia sem - - - - - - - pre, sem - - pre il tuo
be in glo - - - - - - - ry, glo - - ry e -
sem - pre, sem - - - - - pre, sem - pre il tuo
glo - ry, glo - - - - - - ry, glo - ry e -
- - ti - fi - ca - to sia sem - - - - pre il tuo no - - -
- - low'd thy name be in glo - - - - ry e - ter - - -
no - - me, san - - ti - fi - ca - to,
- ter - - nal, hal - - low'd thy name be,
San - ti - fi - ca - - to sia sem - - - - pre il tuo
hal - low'd thy name be in glo - - - - ry e -
21
cresc.
f dim.
ff dim.
no - - me, E lau - - - de e
- ter - - nal; be prais'd, be
no - - me, E lau - - - de e
- ter - - nal; be prais'd, be
- - me, E lau - - - de e
- - nal; be prais'd, be
E lau - de e gra - - - - - zia, e lau - de e
be prais'd, be thank'd, be prais'd, be
no - me, E lau - de e gra - - - - -
- ter - - nal; be prais'd, be thank'd

27
pp
sempre dim.
morendo
gra - - - zia di ciò che ci fai.
thank'd for thy good - ness, thy love.
gra - - - zia di ciò che ci fai.
thank'd for thy good - ness, thy love.
gra - - - zia di ciò che ci fai.
thank'd for thy good - ness, thy love.
gra - - zia di ciò che ci fai.
thank'd for thy good - ness, thy love.
p
zia di ciò che ci fai. Av - ven - ga il
for thy good - ness, thy love. Lord, may thy
34
p
ppp
sic - co - me po - ne
as we im - plore thee
Av - ven - ga il re - gno tuo, sic - co - me po - ne
Lord, may thy king - dom come, as we im - plore thee
Sic - - co - me po - ne Que - -
as we im - plore thee kneel - -
Sic - - co - me po - ne, sic - co - me po - ne
as we im - plore thee, as we im - plore thee,
re - gno tuo, sic - co - me po - ne Que - -
king - dom come, as we im - plore thee kneel - -

40
Que - sta o - ra - zion:
kneel - ing in pray'r:
tua vo - lon - tà si fac - cia,
thy will be done in all things,
cresc.
fac - cia, sic - co - me in cie
in all things, let earth and heav'n
p
f
46
sic co - me in cie
let earth and heav'n

52

sotto voce, dolcissimo

lo, in ter - ra in u - ni - o - ne. Pa - dre,
u - ni - ted bow be - fore thee. Fa - ther,

sotto voce, dolcissimo

lo, in ter - ra in u - ni - o - ne. Pa - dre,
u - ni - ted bow be - fore thee. Fa - ther,

cie - lo, in ter - ra in u - ni - o - ne.
heav'n u - ni - ted bow be - fore thee.

sotto voce, dolcissimo

lo, in ter - ra in u - ni - o - ne. Pa - dre,
u - ni - ted bow be - fore thee. Fa - ther,

sotto voce, dolcissimo

lo, in ter - ra in u - ni - o - ne. Pa - dre,
u - ni - ted bow be - fore thee. Fa - ther,

sotto voce, dolcissimo

59

Pa - dre, dà og - gi a noi pa - ne, e ti piac - cia Che ne per -
fa - ther, each day still sus - tain us. May it please thee, grant us for -

Pa - dre, dà og - gi a noi pa - ne, e ti piac - cia Che ne per -
fa - ther, each day still sus - tain us. May it please thee, grant us for -

sotto voce, dolcissimo

a noi pa - ne, e ti piac - cia Che ne per -
Still sus - tain us. May it please thee, grant us for -

Pa - dre, dà og - gi a noi pa - ne, e ti piac - cia Che ne per -
fa - ther, each day still sus - tain us. May it please thee, grant us for -

Pa - dre, dà og - gi a noi pa - ne, e ti piac - cia Che ne per -
fa - ther, each day still sus - tain us. May it please thee, grant us for -

65
pp
- do - ni, che ne per - do - ni li pec - ca - - ti nos - tri; Nè
- give - ness, grant us for - give - ness when we sin a - gainst thee; and
- do - ni, che ne per - do - ni li pec - ca - - ti nos - tri; Nè
- give - ness, grant us for - give - ness when we sin a - gainst thee; and
- do - ni, che ne per - do - ni li pec - ca - ti nos - tri; Nè
- give - ness, grant us for - give - ness when we sin a - gainst thee; and
- do - ni, che ne per - do - ni li pec - ca - - ti nos - tri; Nè
- give - ness, grant us for - give - ness when we sin a - gainst thee; and
- do - ni, li pec - ca - ti nos - tri; Nè
- give - ness, when we sin a - gainst thee; and
70
dolcissimo
pp
co - sa noi fac - ciam che ti dis - piac - cia.
pur - i - fy our hearts, lest we dis - please thee.
co - sa noi fac - ciam che ti dis - piac - cia.
pur - i - fy our hearts, lest we dis - please thee.
[mp]
co - sa noi fac - ciam che ti dis - piac - cia. E che noi
pur - i - fy our hearts, lest we dis - please thee. May we learn
co - sa noi fac - ciam che ti dis - piac - cia. E che noi
pur - i - fy our hearts, lest we dis - please thee. May we learn
ppp
co - sa noi fac - ciam che ti dis - piac - cia.
pur - i - fy our hearts, lest we dis - please thee.
mp

77
per - do - niam, tu ti di - mo - stri E - sem - - - pio a noi per
to for - give; guide us and teach us like thee to turn from
per - do - niam, tu ti di - mo - stri E - sem - pio a noi per
to for - give; guide us and teach us like thee to turn from
83
o - gnun si
that fear - some
Ac - ciò dal rio ne - mi - - -
that Sa - tan's fear - - some darts
la tua gran vir - tu - - - te;
wrath to love and mer - - - cy;
la tua gran vir - tu - - - te; Ac - ciò dal rio ne -
wrath to love and mer - - - cy; that Sa - tan's fear - - some

88
sotto voce, dolcissimo
schio - - stri, o - gnun si schio - - stri. Di - vi - no
darts may ne - ver reach us. Fa - ther most
- co o - gnun si schio - - stri. Di - vi - no
may ne - ver reach us. Fa - ther most
O - gnun si schio - - - - - stri.
may ne - ver reach us.
mi - - - co o - gnun si schio - - stri. Di - vi - no
darts may ne - ver reach us. Fa - ther most
Di - vi - no
Fa - ther most
93
Pa - dre, pien d'ogni sa - lu - te, An - cor ci guar - da dal - la ten - ta -
ho - ly, thou a-lone canst save us: e - ver pro - tect us; keep us from temp -
Di - vi - no Pa - dre, ci guar - da dal - la ten - ta -
Fa - ther most ho - ly, pro - - tect us; keep us from temp -

99
più piano ancora
-zio - ne, an - cor ci guar - da dal - la ten - ta - zio - ne
-ta - tion; e - ver pro - tect us; keep us from temp - ta - tion;
più piano ancora
-zio - ne, an - cor ci guar - da dal - la ten - ta - zio - ne
-ta - tion; e - ver pro - tect us; keep us from temp - ta - tion;
più piano ancora
-zio - ne, an - cor ci guar - da dal - la ten - ta - zio - ne
-ta - tion; e - ver pro - tect us; keep us from temp - ta - tion;
più piano ancora
-zio - ne, an - cor ci guar - da dal - la ten - ta - zio - ne
-ta - tion; e - ver pro - tect us; keep us from temp - ta - tion;
più piano ancora
-zio - ne, an - cor ci guar - da dal - la ten - ta - zio - ne
-ta - tion; e - ver pro - tect us; keep us from temp - ta - tion;
più piano ancora
104
f
Dell' in - fer - nal ne - mi - co,
guard us from Sa - tan's grasp,
f
Dell' in - fer - nal ne - mi - co, e sue fe -
guard us from Sa - tan's grasp, lest he en -
f
Dell' in - fer - nal ne - mi - co
guard us from Sa - tan's grasp, Lord,
f
Dell' in - fer - nal ne -
guard us from Sa - tan's
f
Dell' in - fer - nal ne - mi - co, e sue fe - ru - te, dell' in - fer -
guard us from Sa - tan's grasp, lest he en - slave us, guard us from
f

110
fff
dell' in - fer - nal ne - mi - co, e sue fe -
guard us from Sa - tan's grasp, lest he en -
- ru - te, dell' in - fer - nal ne - mi - co, e sue fe -
- slave us, guard us from Sa - tan's grasp, lest he en -
e sue fe - ru - te, dell' in - fer - nal ne - mi - co, e sue fe -
lest he en - slave us, guard us from Sa - tan's grasp, lest he en -
- mi - co, dell' in - fer - nal ne - mi - co, e sue fe -
grasp, Lord, guard us from Sa - tan's grasp, lest he en -
- nal ne - mi - co, dell' in - fer - nal ne - mi - co, e sue fe -
Sa - tan's grasp, Lord, guard us from Sa - tan's grasp, lest he en -
116
pp
sotto voce, dolcissimo
- ru - te. Di - vi - no Pa - dre, an - cor ci
- slave us. Fa - ther most ho - ly, e - ver pro -
- ru - te. Di - vi - no Pa - dre, an - cor ci
- slave us. Fa - ther most ho - ly, e - ver pro -
- ru - te. ci
- slave us. Pro -
- ru - te. Di - vi - no Pa - dre, an - cor ci
- slave us. Fa - ther most ho - ly, e - ver pro -
- ru - te. Di - vi - no Pa - dre, an - cor ci
- slave us. Fa - ther most ho - ly, e - ver pro -

123
guar - da dal - la ten - ta - zio - ne, ci guar - - - -
- tect us, keep us from temp - ta - tion; pro - tect
guar - da dal - la ten - ta - zio - ne, Dell' in - fer - nal ne - mi - co, e sue fe -
- tect us, keep us from temp - ta - tion; from Sa - tan's grasp pro - tect, lest he en -
129
ppp portando la voce
- - - - - da; Sì che a te fac - cia - mo o - ra - zi - o - ne, Che
us. There - fore to thee we turn in a - dor - a - tion that
- ru - te; Sì che a te fac - cia - mo o - ra - zi - o - ne, Che
- slave us. There - fore to thee we turn in a - dor - a - tion that
- ru - te;
- slave us.
ppp

135
pppp
me - ri - tiam tua gra - zia, e il re - gno vos - tro A pos - se - der ve -
we may gain for - give - ness, and in thy king - dom rest in peace, we
me - ri - tiam tua gra - zia, e il re - gno vos - tro ve -
we may gain for - give - ness, and in thy king - dom, we
A pos - se - der ve -
may rest in peace, we
141
cresc.
f
- gniam con di - vo - zio - ne. Pre - ghiam - ti, re di glo - -
come in deep de - vo - tion. We name thee King of Glo - -

149
pp [subito]
- ria e si - gnor no - - stro, Che tu ci guar - di da do - lo -
- ry, as Lord a - dore thee, save us, pre - serve us from dam - na -
155
- re: e fit - to La men - te ab - bia - mo in te,
- tion; as firm - ly our faith we fix in thee,
in te, col vol - to pro -
in thee, pros - trate be - fore

Originated by Figaro